W9-CSF-759

Warmed by Love

Other books by

Leonard Nimoy

These Words Are for You
Come Be with Me
We Are All Children Searching for Love

Warmed by Love

A collection of poems by

Leonard Nimoy

Blue Mountain Press ™

Boulder, Colorado

Printed in the United States of America.

Library of Congress Number: 83-071747
ISBN: 0-88396-200-4

First Printing: September, 1983

Thanks to the Blue Mountain Arts creative staff.

Cover photograph by Stephen Schutz.

Blue Mountain Press INC.

P.O. Box 4549, Boulder, Colorado 80306

CONTENTS

INTRODUCTION

I must have been quite a sight driving through Hollywood on a rainy night. Tears were rolling down my cheeks, and I was shouting poetry to no one in particular. It was 1951. I was twenty years old and living 3,140 miles away from my family in Boston, struggling to find work as an actor. Times were bad and work was scarce. Established performers were having difficulty supporting themselves. I was working in an ice-cream parlor to make ends meet and living in a rooming house where the rent was $6 a week in a room for two.

I was an intense young man in love with acting. Looking back, I realize that I probably wasn't very much fun to be around. I was too serious to have much of a sense of humor, and my range of interests wasn't very wide. I had strong opinions on acting, films and theatre. I thought about little else.

The work search process, "looking for a break," was tough. Constant rejection was taking its toll. "You're too young . . . ." "You're the wrong type . . . ." "Not enough experience. . . ." You can't help taking it personally, and your sense of self-worth takes a beating.

On this particular rainy night I was driving home from a movie. I don't even remember what it was. Possibly a Bogart or Cagney film. It was good. So good that I wanted desperately to do work like that. I wanted to be a part of that process that reaches out to touch and entertain and sometimes, hopefully, bring insight and positive change to an audience.

I wanted it so much that the tears began to flow. And then came the words of "Invictus," a poem that I had learned in high school. As I drove and cried, I found myself shouting . . .

Out of the night that covers me,
    Black as the Pit from pole to pole,
I thank whatever gods may be
    For my unconquerable soul.

In the fell clutch of circumstance,
    I have not winced nor cried aloud.
Under the bludgeonings of chance
    My head is bloody, but unbowed.

Beyond this place of wrath and tears
    Looms but the horror of the shade,
And yet the menace of the years
    Finds, and shall find me, unafraid.

It matters not how strait the gate,
    How charged with punishments the scroll,
I am the master of my fate:
    I am the captain of my soul!

It was a defiant cry. It was my way of fortifying myself. Of taking my stand. Of saying . . . . .

> "I will not give up . . .
> I will not be beaten . . .
> I will win . . . ."

Today it seems there was a touch of arrogance in that posture. But I ask forgiveness. Each of us has to find our own way of dealing with those moments of loneliness, helplessness and frustration. My way was a defiant cry of positive strength, even as paratroopers are trained to shout "Geronimo" as they jump out of airplanes. It's a way of driving away the fears that might paralyze us.

Now, some thirty years after that lonely night, I read through the poems in this volume and find the traces of those moments. In **You and I**, I wrote:

> Searching for me,
> I wander
> Through a house of mirrors.
>
> I see a myriad of images,
> But none are mine.
>
> Only distorted reflections
> Of a stranger.
>
> Someone I've met
> But don't really know.
>
> I cry out my name,
> But the hollow echo that responds
> Tells me I must wait.
>
> It is not yet time.

Later, in **Will I Think Of You** I was able to say . . . .

> You were there
> When I came alive
> And discovered my place . . . .

Still later, in **We Are All Children** I rejoiced in the child self which lives within each of us, and the joys of self-worth and commitment to relationships continued in **Come Be With Me** and **These Words Are for You**.

In these writings I've passed through a long and varied road. There have been trials and there have been triumphs. I can only hope the reader can identify with my travels and share the sense of fulfillment that these words represent for me.

Leonard Nimoy
September, 1983

7

The More We Share,
The More We Have

The miracle is this . . .
The more we share
The more
We have.

There is no peace
    Without harmony
No harmony
    Without music

There is no music
    Without song
No song
    Without beauty

There is no beauty
    Without laughter
No laughter
    Without joy

There is no joy
    Without kindness
No kindness
    Without caring

No caring
    Without love
No love
    Without you

Someone
I'm always delighted to see

Someone
 Who is welcome
  to what I have

Who offers
 what I need
Before I even realize
 I need it

Who takes
 easily and gratefully

Who gives
 for the joy
    of it

Who doesn't need
 to keep score

That's you

 my friend

I don't touch you often enough
I don't tell you often enough
That I care about you.

If I were to take the time
To tell you about each time
That I think of you,
  I would spend
  All my time
  Telling you about
    Thinking of you

When I see
The sorrows of the world
  Leaning heavy
    On your shoulders
I wish they were
  On mine instead

  Because,
    I care about you.

Day after day
passes
As I wonder
what next?
What shall I do next?

What shall I begin
to try
to do
to challenge
myself?

Finally,
The answer comes
simply . . .
clearly . . . .

Do something
for someone else . . .
Some surprise
something . . .
Some unexpected
something
Which says,
I thought
of you
I care
about you
I wanted
to do
something
for you . . .

I came to you
Lonely and
Drifting . . .

You taught me
What I'm worth

I came to you
Hungry
And I was fed

I came to you
Needing
And you gave

When I talked,
When I spoke
Of my yearnings
And my dreams . . .
You listened,
And not only listened
You heard.

Will you let me
do
the same
For you?

When you
Let me take
I'm grateful

When you
Let me give
I'm blessed

I know
That there is nothing
In this world
That you wouldn't do
If I asked you to
And I would do
The same for you

So many times
I've thought . . .

  I need
    I want
      someone to help me

  Someone to understand
        to care

  Someone or something
      to soothe this emptiness
        this feeling of being lost

It never works that way

      When I care
      When I help or console
      Or offer understanding
        To someone else

        My own emptiness disappears
          And I am fulfilled

*L*et's do it
All over again
Starting from
The beginning

Let us re-touch
Every step
Along the way

All the joys, fears
Laughter and tears
That brought us as
close
as we are
Today
Let's do it all

All over again

I Guess I'm Just an Old-Fashioned Spaceman

Rocket ships
 Are exciting
But so are roses
 On a birthday

Computers are exciting
 But so is a sunset

And logic
 Will never replace
  Love

Sometimes I wonder
 Where I belong
  In the future
   Or
  In the past

I guess I'm just
 An old-fashioned
  Spaceman

I may not be the fastest
I may not be the tallest
            Or the strongest

I may not be the best
Or the brightest

            But one thing I can do better
            Than anyone else . . .

            That is

            To be me

I have walked alone
  Seeking answers

I have lived alone
  Chasing dreams

I have tried
  To prove my worth
To worthless judges

I have cried my pain
  In silent screams

    I have been
      Sometimes served
      A touch of kindness

    I have wandered   *I have soared*
      In golden fields   *Alone*
          Of grace   *Above the cloud heads*

    I have been   *I have walked*
      Released by honest   *The deep dark*
          Laughter   *Tunnels of the earth*

    I have touched   *I have dined*
      The Western Wall   *With mystics*
      Of the Holy Place   *And with prophets*

                              I have heard
                                The pain of woman
                                Giving birth

                                  I have been
                                    Sought after
                                      As a teacher

                                  I have been
                                    Refused
                                      The Laurel Wreath

                                  I have heard
                                    The thunder blast
                                      Of sunrise

I have watched
The final touch
Of death

I have played
The rules
Set by the master

Though often I didn't
Understand the game

I have worn
More masks than
I remember

I have been
A face without
A name

And when
Like you
I ask
The final question

Who on earth
Am I supposed
To be?

I always
Come full circle
To the answer

Me

Only me

Always me . . .

I have lived with me
for a long time
and plan to continue

*I would like
to keep my friendship
with others*

*But,
I must keep faith
with myself*

*I*f all the deeds of man
  Were grains of sand
And if all those grains
  Of sand were deposited
On a balance scale

  If one side of the scale
   Were the deeds
    Which ennoble humanity
  And the other side weighed
    The deeds which degrade
    The individual

    Would you not
     Count it as a blessing
     To be given the choice
    Each day
      To drop a few grains
      On the side of decency?

So this is the
   Blessed opportunity
   Provided to each of us
      Each day
   To tip the scale
   With a few small grains
   Of kindness
     With a smile
       With a word of encouragement
      A promise kept
       Or an offer of help
        At a moment of need

May you be guided by
The heavenly light

May your dreams
Become solid and sound

May your goals be
Well chosen and surely found

May your deeds be touched
By decency and grace

And above all,
May you find the time
To be kind

*There is a great pleasure
In wanting*

*The object of desire
Seems so perfect
so useful
so necessary
You wonder how you
Ever got along without it
And you know that you must
Have it now*

*Closets full of neglected,
Once desired objects
Tell me that
It was the wanting
That was important*

*I have learned
A precious lesson*

*I have learned
To want
What I have.*

Because
  I have known despair
  I value hope

Because
  I have tasted frustration
  I value fulfillment

Because
  I have been lonely
  I value love

When I truly give
In a love
As the artist gives
In his art
I am fulfilled
Manyfold.

I have learned again
To trust myself

Sometimes . . .
It isn't easy

Sometimes . . .
Someone who seems
to know
Someone who seems
to be wiser
Can convince me,
that I'm on
the wrong path

Not wanting to seem
too stubborn
Not wanting to be
too difficult
And above all
wanting to be
liked . . .

I have occasionally
been persuaded
to leave my own path
to go the way of another
Even when all my instincts
tell me to trust myself

Sometimes it works
but often it doesn't.

And worst of all . . .

Sometimes it's hard
to find my own way again

I'm not always able to give

I'm sometimes empty

And even when
I want to give
Sometimes I can't find
The key to the door of me

And even when I get
The door open
Sometimes
There's nothing there

So please understand
When I can't give

In a little time
I'll be full again

I love to give
And as soon
As I can
I will

Sometimes
Are grey times

Scanning
The overcast sky

Across the tops
Of wet stately pines
I look for the light
Of heaven's rays

Blocked by the
cold grey
of winter clouds

Until at last
thinning to fleece
the moist white
gives way

And

As it has always
been
The darkness lightens

Allowing me
to see through

To the first
patch
of blue

It is time
to give
For I have been given
so much

And now it is time
to give in return

I have seen pleasure
and sorrow
triumph
and defeat

I have seen
the joys of life
and watched
the face of death

I have walked
the road
Which sometimes seemed
unbearably long
hard and unbending

I have seen it
suddenly become
a path of glory
rich
fertile
lush
and giving

Whatever I have passed on
has come back
to me
in word
and deed

Whatever I have given
I have gained

And now
I shall
start the cycle
again

We Are All
Children
Searching
for
Love

I am convinced
That if all mankind
Could only gather together
In one circle
Arms on each other's shoulders
And dance, laugh and cry
             together
        Then much
                of the tension and burden
                        of life
                Would fall away
In the knowledge that
We are all children

Needing and wanting
Each other's
Comfort and
Understanding

We are all children
Searching for love

Love does happen
  Like a touch
    Of grace

    It falls
    Into place
    Where there used
        To be
          Empty space

When I hold your
      face
In my hands
    I ask
How did this happen
      To me?

When love happens
    Through a person or
    A song or a poem

What joy
    What excitement
To know that I
    All of me,
My child and my adult
    All of me,
Is touched again
    With the flowing love
    Of the best that is me
    And my fellow man
       That part of us . . .
          That cares.

You stepped
  Deep into
    The waters
    Of my soul

Patiently you searched
  For the precious
              Stone

You found it
  Warmed it
    Caressed it
And gave it
  To me
Unselfishly
  As a gift

And now
  It is ours
    And we call it
              Love

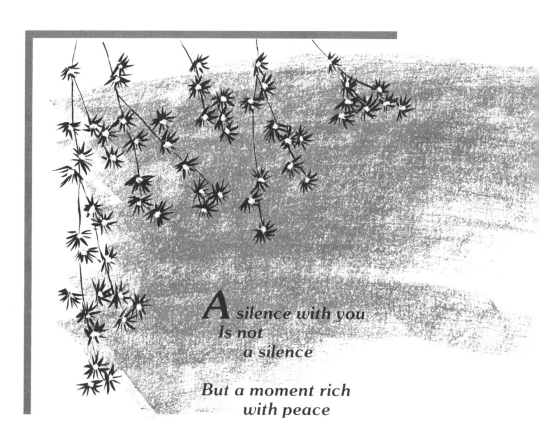

A silence with you
Is not
   a silence

But a moment rich
   with peace

*H*elp me . . .

    Help me
      To say I love you
        Because I do

It should be easy
    To say I love you
    Because
      It's true

        What is this fear
        That ties my tongue
        That locks
          the words
          away inside
          deep inside

Help me
    Turn the key

    Help me
      To speak
      the truth . . .

        Help me to say
        I love you

Like a circle
In the sand
Loneliness waits
For a
Love wind
To wash it
To the sea

I'll be your
wind
Will you be
mine?

There is in me
A being little known
To others
A person,
>   *man or boy*
Locked away

I believe
That he is me

More me
>   *Than the one*
Anyone knows

And that he
Deserves at least
A trial
>   *Before being sealed away*
Forever
>   *Locked inside*
>   *The public face.*

>   *I am still a child*

>   *Thrilled by a sunrise*
>   *Touched by a bird-song*
>   *Delighted by a clown*

>   *Frightened by hatred*
>   *Hurt by rejection*
>   *Saddened by pain*

>   *Warmed by love*

*N*ow spend this day
      with me alone
We'll walk the beach
      and seek the stone
Which when it's found
      will wonders tell
      of magic lands
        and mystic bells

Of ships and sailors
      storms at sea
Of giant serpents
      swimming free

And you and I
      will know once more
      as we drift homeward
      from the shore,
      that we live in
A world sublime

      Two children
      In the strand of time.

Two beings meet

Stand side by side
Young and fearful

Protected by
Layer upon layer
Of defenses

Wanting
To reach
And be reached

Touch
And be touched

Wanting to open
And be opened

Time
Joy
Sorrow
Fear
all pass

And now
You tell me
I'm changed
Mellowed
Easier to be with

And so are you
My child . . .
So are you.

Go, my child
And find your way
Though I would rather
Have you stay

Take now your chance
To reach for more
Than ever I have known
Before

Add not your tears
To those men cried
In mourning
For their dreams that died

Look back, but now and then
To tell
Of where you go
And are you well

This thought to warm you
'gainst the chill
I love you now
And ever will

If I try
To make you believe
That all is good
And will be

    That would be a lie

    And a lie
    Stands between people
    As an invisible wall

    Denying closeness
        For fear that the lie
        Will spring out
        Into the open
          And attack . . .

A lie destroys trust
In oneself
And in each other

No,
   I will not try
   To have you believe
   That all is good

I am too selfish

   I want your love
   And your trust

We are all children
  Seeking the fountain
We are all children
  Washed by the rain

We are the dreamers
  We are the dancers

Life is the music
  Love is the song.

We are all children
Needing laughter
Fighting tears
  Hiding fears

We are all children
Seeking release
Hungry for peace

We are all children
Crossing the ocean
We are all children
Tossed by the storm

Swimming the waters
Of God's devotion
Seeking a harbor to
Offer us home

We are all children
Of various ages

We are all children
The near and the far

Give us the peace
To search not for sages
Give us the strength
To love what we are.

*C*ome,
Let us dance together
sing together.

Let us reawaken
the innocence
the wonder
the simple
Joy and faith
Which is rightfully ours

Let us unburden ourselves
  Of the disguises
    the roles,
    the weights,
    the chains . . .
Which hide and bind
The children
    That we are

For we are,
  All of us —
    Children.

We are the tree
The leaf
The bud
And the blossom

All are part
Of the fruit
Of God's love

Our love for one
Is our love
For all

And if you take from me
I am blessed
For in the exchange
I am no longer
Alone.

We are the players
And the game

We are the remembered
And the forgotten

We are the prize
And the loss,
The sweet,
And the bitter.
The accident
And the choice.

Each of us is Pawn
And King.

We are the miracle
  And the salvation

We are the expected
We are the past
      Present
          And always

We are the faith
  And the faithful

We are the leaders
  And the led

We are the masters
We are the slaves
      We are the beginning
          And the end

We are the storm
      And we are the calm
The ocean
      And the shore

We are each
      And we are all
We are every one
      The great
      And the small

We are the earth
We are the heavens

We are yesterday
          And tomorrow
We are the father
          And the son
          The giver
          And the given
There is no better
          And no worse

So let us rejoice
      Let us sing
      Jump,
            Clap,
And dance to the music
For we are the music,
            The words
            And the dance

            We are all.

*W*e are the poem
      And the poet
We are the words
      The paper
And the print

For we are here
      Together
In the circle
      Touching
And touched

We are the laughter
      And the tears

Who is it that sings?
It is us
Who is it that cries
Out?
It is us
Who is it that
Stumbles and falls
Then runs free
In the field?
It is us

Then let us know it
Let us drink it
Let us praise it
Let us savor it
Let us thank each other

Let us ride the wave
To the crest
Of life

To take part
In the all
That we are

Let us sit on the
 Top of the hill
  in darkness
Watching and waiting
  in the sure
And blessed
   knowing
That the sun
 which has been
 Elsewhere
Visiting with
 the others
 of us
Will soon
 be here
To warm our chill
 To lighten our way
  To embrace the all
  That we are

Let us give thanks
for the
Eternal spring
of love, Hallelujah!
Which is within us, Hallelujah!

The love we have
searched for
The love that is
ours
The love that is
The children
we are

Let us say
Hallelujah!
Amen

You and I

In my heart
Is the seed of the tree
Which will be me.

Nourished by understanding
Warmed by friends
Fed by loved ones
Matured by wisdom
Tempered by tears.

PATIENCE . . .

The seasons pass,
The seed sprouts.
The young branches begin to form,
To reach out for new experiences,
New contacts,
To test their strength
In the wind.
To examine their size and shape
As a child discovers
Its own hands and feet.

Speed is glory.
Speed is fame and fortune.
Speed is a gold medal.
Speed is honor.
Speed is success.

Speed is a thief.

Some rush about in preparation.
Some struggle to be nearest to the gate.
Some climb to be at the highest place.
And yet,
            we shall all be born,
All will move about
In time
And space.

Life comes and goes.

Laughter of the past
Rings through empty hallways.

The seasoning is bittersweet.

Searching for me,

I wander
Through a house of mirrors.

I see a myriad of images,
But none are mine.

Only distorted reflections
Of a stranger.

Someone I've met
But don't really know.

I cry out my name,
But the hollow echo that responds
Tells me I must wait.

It is not yet time.

I am not alone.
There are times when I think I am,
Feel like I am
Alone and lost.
But as the river bends,
And the drifting traveler
Sees the unfolding of new vistas,
New Horizons,
New landmarks,
I find a new communion
With the turn of time,
A new sense of
Universal connection.

And then . . .
One day in the spring of my life
The buds and the blossoms appear

I am alive

I am here

I have joined the earth
Like a tidepool . . .
Filled by the mist
And the great waves.
Giving of myself
To the air and the earth.
Living at peace
With the sun and moon.
Cousin to the fog and rain.

The melody is simple

and the words are sweet.

I am not immortal.

Whatever I put off for later
May never be.

Whoever doesn't know now
That I love them
May never know.

I have killed time.
  I have squandered it.
    I have lost days . . . weeks . . .
As a man of unlimited wealth
Might drop coins on the street
And never look back.
I know now, that there will be an end,
A limit.
  *But there **is** time*
  Valuable and precious time
  To walk,
      talk,
        breathe.
  Time to touch,
        taste,
          care.
  To warm the child
  Who is cold and lonely.
  There is time to love
  I promise myself . . .
            I will.

I am.
I am ready.
I am ready to give.
I am ready to give and to receive.
I am ready to give and to receive love.

How will I know her?

I will know her by
Her being,
By her aura.
Though she be
A glimpse
A flash,
My eye will know.

I will know her.
Even if she comes
In the darkness
Of the darkest night
Her fragrance . . .
Will sing to me.

Even if her sound
Should be a whisper
My ear will know.

I will know her.
Even if we
But brush past
Each other in the crowd
Her touch will call
To my brain . . .
She is here!

How will she know me?

If she is ready . . .
She will know me.

I will search for you.

I know that you
Will be searching too.

I will watch for you
As I watch the day break,
The sun set.

I will listen for you
In the singing of the river,
The mating of the tree branches.

And if we keep our hearts open
Surely we shall pass through
The doors of loneliness
Into the warmth of love.

I watch,

I listen,

I wait.

High, high up on a hill
In a house of ruby glass
Living in the warmth
Of the sun

Lives the love I look for.

In a ruby glass house
Without a door,
Burning, reflecting
From the eye of my desire.

At times
I hold my breath.
Did I hear a sound?
Was there a signal?

I must be patient.

Morning comes
When night is done.

Burn all your candles.
Light all your lamps
Between sunset and dawn.
It is still night.

Today,
Time has stopped.

A minute is still a minute.
An hour is still an hour.

And yet,

The past and the future
Hang in perfect balance.
All focused on the present.

A sweet flow of excitement
Warms me.

You are near.

         You are here.

But
you seem unsure.

Are you ready?
Do you know me?

You seem unsure . . .

Do I offer too little,
Or is it too much?

You seem unsure.

Am I too late,
Or is it too soon?

I have known you for a thousand years,
In other times and other worlds

I have known your heart,
Your mind and your very soul.

We have traveled separately,
Through endless space and time
To be together here.

I have always known
That it would come to pass.

I have watched and waited.

I could enter a crowded room
And in an instant
Know that this was not
The time nor the place.

And now . . .
        Today . . .
I hear a sound . . .
And I know . . .
I sense your presence . . .
       And I know . . .

Your questions touch me.
You ask:

Will it always be easy?
Will it be forever?

I wish I could answer yes . . .
I can only say

Let's begin
to try
to do
to build
to breathe
to live

with patience

with care

with an open mind.

Let us join the ages.

The tides flow.
The sun rises and sets.
The seasons come and go.
The moon and the stars
light the night way
For each of us.

What we plant today
Will root and grow.

Let us plant a seed,
Love and protect it
Feed and warm it.

Surely a tree will rise
to take its place in the sun

Let us plant today
The seed which will be
The tree of us . . .

Yes,
you are.

I understand because
I am too.

Each of us exists
separate and alone.

This is your Spring,
your precious time
to blossom,
to be.

Will you be with me?

And now
at last,

We are.

Side-by-side,

Together-opposed,

In spite of each other,

Because of each other.

In the midst of lies and painful sorrows
Lonely men without tomorrows
Promises not meant for keeping
Curtains drawn but not for sleeping
On top of the mountain stand
You and I.

The eye of time looks on in wonder
The circus band blares out its number
Grey heads sitting in the sun
Wond'ring what they might have done
In the vortex stand
You and I.

In the rushing,
        crushing
                pell-mell dashing
Flow of moments going by
Blowing winds and falling leaves
Swaying trees that bend and sigh
Prayers floating, hearts emoting
In the center ring stand
You and I.

Move slowly,

       Oh so slowly.

Make time stand still.

       I wake up to

       A warm wet sunrise

       Where my love lies

              I am deeply moved
              by a shaft of sunlight
              breaking through the trees,
              by a piece of music
              drifting out of a passing car,
              the sandpipers on the beach
              running to and fro,
              playing tag with the surf
              because of you . . . .

I can think back on times when
I thought I saw
Thought I heard
Places I've visited
But didn't really experience.

I am a child.
I look forward to each new day
With a sense of adventure
There is so much to learn . . .
Because of you . . . .

Your presence
Brings peace to my heart.

Your touch
Is the warmth of the sun.

I walk softly
Through the valley of our love.
Carefully — I avoid crushing
The smallest leaf or branch.
It is alive.
It is precious.
It is holy.
All the great mysteries are resolved.
All the great questions are answered.

But . . .
The way of love
Is so fragile . . . .

Last night . . .

I held you not so close to me
Being only half convinced
That you were where you wanted to be.

You held me in a half sure way,
Sensing my indecision.

Oh my darling,

    today

        all day —

        I thought of you

My being is broken
with pain beyond bearing.

        Is there anything left behind
        When the sun disappears?

        Is there anything left behind
        When the morning dew dries?

        Is there anything left behind
        When words lead to tears?

        Is there anything left behind
        When a love dies?

I have been alone before
And thought I knew loneliness.
I was wrong.

There were three:

You and I,
        and we.

        Without you there is
        less than one.

Tonight . . .

> *You were crying*
> *And it hurt me*
>
> *I was angry*
> *Because I felt guilty*
>
> *We talked*
> *We argued*
> *We cried*
>
> *We held each other*
>
> *We cried*
>
> > *together*

I hope it rains . . .
I'll walk in it and get soaked.

The day is filled with exquisite beauty
Surging in from all directions.

I see with new eyes
Hear with childlike ears
And my heart is full of joy and wonder.
My only sadness comes
From knowing what has been lost,
The precious time
Which passed while I was asleep.
But even this is washed away
By the richness of now
And the promise of tomorrow

I hope it rains.

I want to shout it in the streets

Wake up!   Life is here!   Live it!

Listen to the music
The rhapsody, the symphony
That surrounds you.

Yet each must find it
In his or her own way.
In their own time
The awakening, the blossoming

Those who find it are blessed
They carry a special aura
A look of beauty and insight
Peace and wisdom.

I like myself . . .
Because of you.

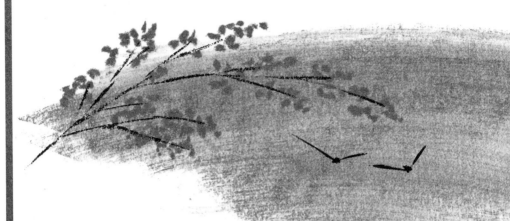

What is old?
Cold is old — a lie is old
Hunger is old — pain is old.

What is young?
The truth is young — love is young.
The sun is young.

It has just occurred to me
That you are young.
And will always be childlike. . .
   And I love you.

What mark will I leave behind?
How will anyone ever know I've been here?
What sign will tell the future traveler
that I existed?
Shall I carve it on a door?

"I am here!

Today . . .

I exist"

I believe the deepest impression is made
In those moments when I can say

I Care.

I Love.

LOVE

From me —— to you

My beauty — take my hand
I'm so proud of you
The way people love you
The strength you offer
To those in need.

I am an incurable romantic
I believe in hope, dreams and decency.

I believe in love,
Tenderness and kindness.

I believe in mankind.

I believe in goodness,
Mercy and charity
I believe in a universal spirit
I believe in casting bread
Upon the waters.

I am awed by the snow-capped mountains
By the vastness of the oceans.

I am moved by a couple
Of any age — holding hands
As they walk through city streets.

A living creature in pain
Makes me shudder with sorrow
A seagull's cry fills me
With a sense of mystery.

A river or stream
Can move me to tears
A lake nestling in a valley
Can bring me peace.

I wish for all mankind
The sweet simple joy
That we have found together.

I know that it will be.

And we shall celebrate
We shall taste the wine
And the fruit.

Celebrate   the sunset and the sunrise
the cold and the warm
the sounds and the silences
the voices of the children.

Celebrate the dreams and hopes
Which have filled the souls of
All decent men and women.

We shall lift our glasses and toast
With tears of joy.

Will I Think of You?

Will I think of you?

Only at sunrise
            Which is God's beginning

For you were there
            At the beginning of me

When I came alive
            And discovered my place

My worth
            The beauty of earth

And the miracle of daybreak
            Once again

And the richness of mornings
            To come

Only In The Morning

Each time
      The darkness of past
Is chased
      By the light of now

                  Will I think of you . . . .
                  Only then

Only at night
　　　　Where the silence

And the blackness
　　　　is touched occasionally
By a lonely cat
　　　　Or suspicious puppy
A passing plane
　　　　red eye winking
To the stars
　　　　Who refuse to be seduced

　　　　When I hear
　　　　　　Your whispered love
　　　　in the tree rustle
When I feel your secret hand
　　　　exploring me
　　　　　　drifting across my skin
To rest in a friendly
　　　　harbor

　　　　And my mind tells me
　　　　I am alone

　　　　But my heart knows better

　　　　Only then

　　　　　　will I think

　　　　　　　　Of you

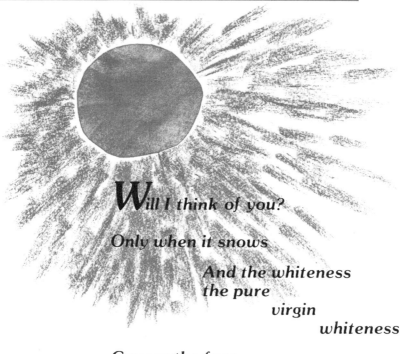

Will I think of you?

Only when it snows

       And the whiteness
       the pure
            virgin
               whiteness

Covers the face
       of the earth
       To cleanse the trampled
          corruption
            Of times past

Like a new love
       delicate

Untracked
       Unexplored

Waiting for the lovers
       To choose carefully
       The path to heaven
          Together

When I am overcome by
        The realization that you
        created the whiteness and the
                        purity

And you led me
        Like a child
                both of us children

Into
        A new and pure

        Wonderful land of our own

Where each step
        Left a priceless
                        landmark

And promised a new
Place to explore
A new step to come

                Then I will
                        Watch the snow
                falling in swirls and flurries
                Of perfect crystal tears

I will watch
The new virginity
                embrace the earth
                        And I will think of you

Only when it rains

I will recall
    An aching soul
    and a crying heart
    standing in pools
    of the saddest light

Back to back
    And moving away
And I knew
    the tears in your heart
Would soon be on your cheeks

        To wet my fingers
        As I held your face
        Up to the light
        To remember
        For tomorrow

                Then . . . .

            Whenever the eyes of heaven
            Overflow
            And God's tears
            Wash across
            My window
            I shall see again
            Those streaks of love
            Which flowed for me
            To bind
            An aching soul
            To a crying heart

                    And I will think of you

And when the day is clear

> *After a rain*
> *And a new vision*
Of the landscape
> *Is visible to all*
> *Who will*
> > *Bother to look*
> > *And see*

> > *When I remember how I felt*
> > *Safe enough*
> > > *With you*
> > > > *To let you*
> > > > *See me*

> > > > > > *Cry*

When the tears
> *washed clean*
The windows of my vision
And I could see
> *The past and present of*
Myself
> *And find hope and strength*
For the future

> > *And after the rain of my crying*
> *I felt washed*

> *And fresh and loved*
> *As my babyself*
> *Must have felt*

> *When my mother*
> *bathed her infant*

> *Then after each rain*
> > *How*
> > > *Can I help*
> > > > *But think of you*

Will I think of you?

> *Only when it's cold*
And I'm shivering
> *Against the wind*

And suddenly from inside
> *The core of me*
> > *From my deepest depths*
Comes
> *A small warming flame*
Which wants to grow
And I fight it
> *Until I realize I need it*

Want it
> *to flow through me*

To fill me
> *Because*
> > *It is you*

Only In The Spring

When the first warm breezes of April
Give courage
  To the youngest
    tenderest
Shoots of nature
  to appear
  to live
   to grow

When the thaw
   in the mountains
Sends the pure cold
   Cascading
   waters
Down the
  hillside
   To fill the streams

As you fill me
   To laughter
   And tears

   Only then . . .

    Will I think of you

Will I think of you?

*Only when I feel
   warmed and wanted*

*Though once
   I felt I was outside
   looking in
   disconnected
Watching the world
   go by*

then . . . .

*I'll remember
   That in your love
   I found acceptance*

And I'll think of you

Only when I laugh

*At a joke of others
   or my own*

Or a memory of you

*And the laughter rises
   Out of the well of me*

*To be tasted
   By my mouth and lips*

When the tickle rolls
through my body

To remind me
Of days and nights
Of free laughter with you

Even while others stared
At the crazy couple
wondering what could be so funny
In a world
Of grim rushing

and painful waiting

Urgent hoping
And sad silences

Then
When the laughter
Is multiplied
By past joys remembered
And I can't stop
Even to catch my breath
Or to give relief to my aching sides

I'll realize
That the laughter of my life
Is for you,
because of you

And I'll think of you

But only then

Or when I'm sad
        and lost
Tired of trying

When the tears and pains
    Of the world
All seem to be mine

When there is no one but you
Who would really understand
The emptiness of my soul
    The sorrow
Of trying
    And failing

        Of knowing that
        Life can be a trial

        Where the judge and jury
Sometimes sit
With faces of stone
    And will not respond
    Even to a cry
    From the truest heart

        When I know
        That the final precious blossom
        Clinging to the tree
          Will surely fall
          Under the constant
          Persistent
          Pressing of the wind

When I know that you
And only you
>*Could see all this*
>*And hear all this*
And be with me
>*In my sadness*
In silent understanding

And shed tears
>*for my sorrow*

Then

>*I will think of you*

>>*Only when the turn of fortune*
>>*Comes my way again*

>>>*When I ride*
>>>*The crest of triumph*
>>>*glowing with pride*
>>>*In the promise fulfilled*

>>>*When the adoring crowd*
>>>*has returned*
>>>*With shouts of approval*

>>*Then I will search*
>>*Their faces*
>>*Looking for the one*
>>*Who stood beside me*
>>*In defeat*
>>*And should be there*
>>*In the victory*
>>*Which is empty*
>>>*Without you*

*W*ill *I think of you?*

No . . . .

Only when I'm with others.

Surrounded
         In a crowded
                 party room

Listening to
         Several conversations

People communicating
         Or trying to . . .

Watching the
         Blur of figures and
Faces go past
         none coming into focus

Except yours

         Again and again
In each corner
In each chair
         In every smile

Only you
         persistent
                 forever

                 Only then

Will I think of you?

   Only on the highway

     When I travel

   Searching for money and fame

   And finding that neither feeds me

When I pass
   The other travelers
     Some going my way
And some not

  But I realize
That this
  Is what we all
Must do . . .

   To fall behind
The traveling flow
   And catch up
And pass others
   Then fall behind again
Passed by those
   Who rush on
Believing that
   It is best
To be there first

  But I know that this is
Where we all are

   On the highway

   That there is no "here" or "there" . . . .
    There is only
      The coming and going

If we can help
One
Who finds the way
Too hard or too long
  Then that is worth
  All of being
And I will try to help

  Because someone helped me

Someone who cared more
About the brothers on the
Road
  Than about the
          Gifts at the end
And that someone was you

      So I will think of you

Only on the beach
  Where the timeless
    Never ending surge
Of water
  Changes
The face of earth
  Again and again
Each minute of the day
           night
           and always

Where the children
And the aged
Come together
To chase a wave
The surf
Of a dream

Where the tide shifts constantly
Teaching me
  That today is only today
And whatever I have
      Good or bad
      Much or little
  Must change
      Or it will rot
      and die

Then and there when I recall
The change
   In this thing called me
The new sides
   New forms
    New shapes of me

Which came
   When you
   Washed across
My being

Then, there
     On the beach
         I will think

       Of you

Will I think of you?

Only when I'm alone

Staring out my window

Into space . . .

> *Which becomes you*

Your love
Smiling back
> *To the warmth*
> *Of my heart*

Filling the emptiness
> *The loneliness*
>> *With your being*

Only then,

> *Will I think of you*

Only when I hear music

    And the songs
    Of the poet singers
        remind me
That
        all things are for all
                people

    That there is
A love and a sorrow
    A joy and a pain
Which each of us separately
Feels
    As if it is ours alone

And it is only ours
Even while it is everyone's

        For each of us is
           A separate miracle
        In a collective miracle

        Brought together
        For a moment
           By a group of notes
        And a scan of words

        From the heart
        Of one
           Who dares
              To think

    That others
    Might feel
        As he feels

And he sings it out to us
*   as a gift*

To be accepted
*   Or rejected*

*   But given with*
*   A heart of love*

I thank them
*   the poet singers*

Who give us communion

And help us join with
*   Each other*
*   think of each other*

And bless us
*   With each other's love*

*   For in that music—love—rhythm*

*   I feel your*
*   Heart beat*

And I will think of you

Will I think of you?

Only when we're apart

And the aching joy-pain of our love

Surrounds me
  Filling the air I breathe

Only with each blink of my
    Eye which yearns
    To re-open to find you here
    With me

Only with
    Each clock-tick
Which makes my ear perk up
Hopeful
    That it has heard
    Your key in the door

Only when I day dream and
                    re-dream

Our coming together again

When the world will fall away
    leaving only two figures

          Yours and mine

Merged into
        A classic chord

          Loving . . .

              Being loved
                In each
                    part of harmony

Only
   When I die

   And realize
   That I am born again

   For dying is

      A beginning
      And I
            have died
                  thousands of times

                  Sometimes
                  Several times a day

I am learning
That from each death
   Comes a new vision
Of life

   A new sense of the miracle
   Of being and creation
For fear
   Is worse than dying . . .

Fear prevents discovery
   And destroys the creative flow
   Of God-man's soul

And when I let my old self
   Hardened and rigid
                Die

I am re-born
   Vital, open and fresh
And this discovery
   This victory over the
                Fear of death
                     Came

When I thought I was dead
   And found you

So
Each time
I rise
Out of the ashes
Of my fear
I will gratefully

                Think of you

Only on Special Days

Birthdays, Holidays

And other days. . . .

When those who
   Give to each other
    And live for each other

     Travel
      For hours or days
       Or for an instant

   To hold
    Or dream-hold
  Each other

To exchange
  Heart-warmth
   And body-warmth

When we commemorate

And Celebrate

   The Special days
  Of a life of love

Then and especially then

Because the day is special
As your glorious being
   Is special
    I will think of you

Only when we're together

And I can think of nothing else
And everything else
Because we together
Are everything
And our togetherness is
All things

Then as always
And forever
I will think of you

*Thank You
    for Your Love*

Sweet is
 The sunbreak
 After the rain

Welcome is
 The breeze
 That follows the heat

Warm is
 The fire
 Against the snow

Yet none
 So precious
 As your smile
That says

 Welcome home . . .

 After we've
 Been apart

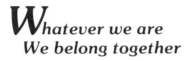

*Whatever we are
We belong together*

*Wherever we are
We will find each other*

*Whoever we are
We are
Forever one*

Yₒu are my ground
You are my base
   My island

You are my safety
   And my warmth

You are my harbor
   With you I am safe
      And at peace

I can be social
   And make small talk
But the truth is,
      I'm shy

You are my haven
   And my retreat

   I may act secure
   And self-assured
   But I'm human . . . .

   I have my moments
   Of self-doubt
   And I can be hurt
      Just like anyone else

You are my firm ground
   You are my strength
   You are
      my love.

These words are for you
To have,
To hold
To keep from now on
Forever.

I love you,
Need you.
I need your laughter
I need your love
Need your warmth

Because,
I care about you
and
I love you

My love is a garden

You are the sun

When you shine
On my garden
It grows

You feed it
With your smile

You warm it
With your heart

You bless it
With your being

When friends say,
My, you have a
beautiful garden

I look at you,
and smile.

You are the dream
I dream

You are the sun
I seek

You are
My shade

You are the rest
I sleep

You are the peace
I yearn for

You are
My hope,
My love

I love to sit with you
At dusk
To watch the day
Withdraw . . .

Night is coming
But,
Before it does
A crack opens
Like a doorway
Between two worlds

Hand in hand
We slip inside
Traveling through
Unknown reaches
On voyages of wonder

Weightless . . .
We leap and bound
Over magic mountains
Through soft mists
Into rich purple valleys
Flying free
Toward the horizon

In a moment
We have lived
A lifetime

Returning
Just in time
To ease through
The doorway
As night closes

*S*_{oft} *. . .*
　The dream of you
　　　Steals across
　　　My sleep
　And whispers
　　　Wake to me
　　　Wake
　　　　to
　　　　　me

I whisper back
　　Your love
　And we sing
　　　Our song
　　　Silently
　　　　Secretly

Until the morning light
　　　Tells us
　　　　It is time

I awake
　Fulfilled
　Stirring from
　　Our night dream
　　To begin
　　　Our daydream

When I am working hard
At something I love
Time goes too fast

When I am doing something
I am not happy doing
It takes forever

When I'm waiting for you
Time goes too slowly

When I'm with you
*   Time disappears*

*F*or the times
When I said things
I shouldn't have
   I'm sorry

For the times
When I did things
I shouldn't have done
I ask you to
   Forgive me

I find no pleasure
In giving you pain
It makes me feel better
To make you feel good.

Let me not take for granted
An act of kindness
An offering of love
The glory of human courage
A sign of respect
A phrase of beautiful music
A decent soul
The beauty of a blossom
And above all,
You.

You mean so much
                to me
I wish
        I could be
A cushion following you
    Wherever you go
    To be there
            In case you should fall.

I won't do that.

    It would deprive you
    Of your self-respect
    But please,
        If there is a bruise,
        Let me help to heal it.

When you touch me
I am deeply touched
Far deeper than the
Depth of skin or flesh

You touch the core
The secret cave
Of my being

You touch the dream place
That some call heart
Some call soul

For me
It has no name
But me
When you touch me
You touch
Me

If the sun turns cold

If the night is too dark,
long and lonely

Try me.

If your trust
has been betrayed

If dreams won't
come true

When hopes seem
to crumble
and fade
to dust

Try me.

If your sadness
leaves a void

An emptiness
which can't
be filled
Except
by love

Try me.

In the desert
    I learned about heat

In the snow
    I learned about cold

    When you left
       I learned about lonely

Without others
    I am
       Alone

Without you
    I am
       Lonesome

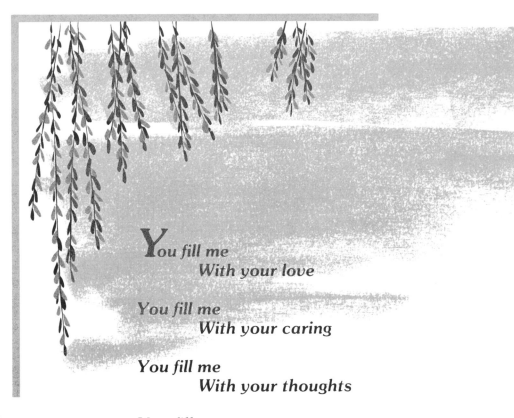

You fill me
   With your love

You fill me
   With your caring

You fill me
   With your thoughts

You fill me
   With your sharing

Where will
There ever be
A space
So full
As that
Which is filled
By our love?

Away and alone
I fill the room
With thoughts
   Of you
   And other times
   In green fields
      Of love remembered
      And cherished . . .

What shall I send you
Across the sea?
   A moment of sweet silence
   Reaching to soul depths
      In hopes of touching
      Your being
         With my mind

I send you this
   My love
These words,
   These special words
   To warm you
      While I'm gone

      Take them to you
      Hold them
         In your heart

   My love is for you
   My love is you

      Take these secret words
      That open doors
         To sacred places
            Known only by lovers
            Such as us.

Come

> *Be with me*

> *Let your mind*
> > *Float free*
> *Across the space*
> > *Of our separation*

Let it join
> *With mine*
For an eternal
> *Moment*

> *Who are better*
> > *Joined?*
> *Those who are together*
> *Each thinking*
> > *Of other people*
> > *In other places*

Or we
> *Who are in other places*
> *Thinking of each other*

> *We are star met*
> *we are joined*
> *we are blessed*
> *we who have found each other*
> *we are the dream of the ages*
> *we are the hope, the desire*
> *we are love*

I'll be with you
          soon

To share
   The seasons
      passing

The crisp of fall
The bud of spring

I'll bring
       You

Kisses,
   Caresses . . .
      Aged by timeless longing

Eye to eye
   Hand in hand
     We'll whisper
       softly
Of Our Love

There have been times
When I thought
I've seen it all
I've done it all before.

And yet tonight
When I saw the sunset
It felt so new
So . . . first time

And now,
When I see again
In your eyes
Your love for me
I'm as touched
As I was
When it all began

Some things
Bear repeating.

I want to see you again
To hold your hand
To touch your face
To feel the earth stand still again
I want to breathe with you
As one again
Not just now and then
But always

I *have seen*
the beauty of love
in your face

I have met
the joy of existence
in your being

I have found
the eternity of life
in your presence

I have touched
the fulfillment
Of perpetual grace

And it is you
all of it
is you

I *love*
To see you
Play the child . . .
Alive
Excited
Hopeful
Dreaming . . .
Forever
The optimist
Forever
Entranced
By a new thought
A new idea . . .

I hope
That I can go on
Forever touching
Those ideas
That awaken
The child in you

You and I have had our share
of laughter
and our share of sadness
our share of good and bad times

and we have our share
of those sweet and precious times
when we seem to blend
into one being
and I am so filled with happiness
that my eyes overflow

some would say these times
are stolen moments

I disagree

I think we've worked for them
I think we've earned them

We started with love
And when our love
Was sometimes shaken
We braced it
With understanding
To give it strength

And when our dreams
Were sometimes shattered
We picked up the pieces
And carefully put them
Together

Binding them with patience
And time . . .
We nursed each other
Through defeat
And learned
To be graceful
In triumph
And now,

We are twice blessed
We are still lovers
And we are friends

If there is
Nothing more than this
  It is enough

We have flown
   The heights

We have rested
  On the crest

We have seen
  The sights of wonder
  The glorious days
  The peaceful nights

We have touched and traveled
Deep into time
  And far beyond the stars

For we have loved
  And who
    Can ask for more?

I love you
Not for what
I want you to be
But for what you are

I loved you then
For what you were
I love you now
For what you have become

I miss you
And not only you

I miss what I am
When you are here...

Take these words
For they are yours

Take these thoughts
For what else
Can I give?

What more can I give
Than the thought
That you are
Loved

Take this love
For who else
Could I give it to
But you

My love for you is not a gift
 To you
  It is a gift
   To me

Thank you
For a world
of kindness

Thank you
For your endless
patience

Thank you
For your sensitive
understanding

Thank you
For your
Love